The

The Modern

Professional

8 hours a week to a more fulfilled and flexible life

By Dr Uche Aniagwu MBBS MSc BSc

Table of Contents

Dedication

This is my second book and I am grateful to say that the experience grows no less riveting and fulfilling. As always, I wouldn't be able to accomplish my goals without my fantastic support system. Multiple times throughout this process I faced challenges and wanted to give up. Despite the values, I preach in this book I still often face trials that test my own principles. I cannot underplay the value of having the right people around me. So, I want to give them a mention for their special contribution towards me writing this book:

Mum

Dad

Olaiya

Tooch

Nam

Ije

Chi Chi

Introduction - The Journey

As an NHS doctor, my life for the most part, was filled with conflicting emotions – a love-hate relationship in its most toxic form. I loved my job. I loved the job that I had trained for the best part of a decade to do and, having been a person with experience in other industries, I could appreciate that the job was better than most. But, like an abusive relationship with some inexplicable dependence, I felt neglected, unheard, overworked and severely underpaid for the sacrifice that I had made and indeed, continue to make. Each day had a similar cycle; I'd go into work feeling tired and wanting the day to end, I'd go full throttle and actually not notice the day go by, then on the way home I'd buy something unhealthy to eat; finally I'd reach home and the reality of physical and social neglect would set in. This is the story of many of us who are healthcare professionals. Although I loved my job, I started to resent aspects of hospital life and decided that I wanted to have more control over some of the essential aspects of my life, but there wasn't an obvious path.

So, what do you do when you don't have a plan? You hope. And that's exactly what I did. I hoped that by progressing up the ladder things would just magically get better. Well, I hoped until I discovered the reality. The reality was that even at more senior levels, you still have an extraordinarily high workload, with even more responsibility, plus growing home responsibilities such as children and large financial commitments. Yes, it's safe to say that realising this, I knew I couldn't continue in this vein any longer. As such, I decided to take a year out after my second year as a doctor. I wasn't sure what the year would have in store, but I absolutely loved the idea of having more control over my working pattern and earning more money. I couldn't understand why everyone wouldn't want to try it, that is until I did it!

To begin my year out of training I worked four on-call shifts per week, mainly at night, and used the proceeds from that to help me run my injectable aesthetics business I had set up the year before. In all fairness, I was pretty used to this since as a second-year doctor I did locums during all my rota gaps so I could pay the rent for my treatment room.

I vividly remember in 2017 when I first heard about injectable aesthetics; the idea of offering Botox and Dermal Fillers had excitement coursing through my veins. I heard all the embellished success stories and how everyone who did it was rich! I was very much part of the boom of healthcare professionals who had decided to take this route to supplement their income and, in the end, it represented a financial drain that led me to work even more in the hospital! Needless to say, the industry wasn't just waiting to give me money and liberate me from my distorted body clock. Goodness! What a shocker! I wouldn't be a millionaire overnight. Excuse the sarcasm but looking back I realise how misguided and naive I was.

Back to the year out – yes, I had more control and money, but I was still working just as hard and not actually gaining any added feeling of fulfilment. I still had not been able to create more time for myself without it having a major impact on my pocket. It was around Christmas

2018 that I sat back and thought, there must be a way to keep doing my job in the NHS but also be able to have an increased sense of fulfilment and generate more money without increasing the time I spend at work. When I would discuss this with my peers, they often looked at me as though I were crazy and politely offered their support while mildly suggesting maybe it was time I accepted reality and squarely faced the life I had signed up for. But you see, I was ignorant to a fault, so what did I do? I started to plot and scheme.

The Life You Want to Live

On the quest for generating an income without slogging long hours at the hospital I asked myself the following questions:

Can I make more money without having to sacrifice sleep and work all hours?

Can I create time for myself and a potential alternative career path that still leverages my qualifications?

Can I do something where I can be influential?

Can this allow me the time to keep my job and be around my family?

Do any of those questions resonate with you? I didn't have the first idea of how I was going to accomplish this, but I did know that I had a medical degree, a clinic room for injectable treatments and some prior knowledge on running successful start-ups. So, I went to my drawing board and started to pen down ideas that could allow me to achieve my goals. I knew that being a regular aesthetician or regular doctor was not going to bring me the life I wanted without an incredible amount of effort and possibly a decade of graft. After much deliberation I came to this conclusion:

Can I make more money without having to sacrifice sleep and work all hours?

Yes, because I will generate high paying opportunities.

Can I create time for myself and a potential alternative career path that still leverages my qualifications?

Yes. I was going to build around my strength. I was a doctor.

Can I do something where I can be influential?

Yes. Injectable aesthetics was saturated with doers, but not many thought leaders or specialists.

Can this allow me the time to keep my job and be around my family?

I was planning to work less than I had ever done.

Now, I'm not going to take complete credit for the plan I'm about to share with you. I had come across these principles in various places before and I was very sceptical of the efficacy of the strategy. So, naturally, I decided to do a quick review of super successful individuals across a range of industries and I noticed a pattern. This wasn't about building super businesses, it was all about building an expert brand that brought some of the perks of building a super business, without the same stress. More importantly, it was about building expert recognition in a world where most obvious things had established experts and you had to be able to find where you fit in. I even went as far as looking at some of my friends, including a young property investor who had many aspects of the life I wanted. To my surprise, the pattern was appearing to repeat itself. I wondered, could it be that all these people had consciously used this plan in order to build clout and expert status around their names? What's more, the thought leaders who came up with these strategies stressed how little time commitment it took to elevate one's self and create entirely new financial abundance. This was a step away from the notion that working the hardest equalled getting the best results. This was about working the smartest. Many of us know that working your arse off does not guarantee the lifestyle you aspire to. Do you think the first billionaire that comes to your mind works 1,000 times harder than you? My point exactly.

8 Hours A Week Is All It Takes

Anyway, I've built enough suspense around what this strategy is; it's time I let you in.

The strategy can be summarised as this:

1. Find your niche
2. Build your pitch
3. Publish in that space
4. Create a product / service
5. Proliferate a consistent profile
6. Collaborate

These, my dear friends, are the six simple steps. I will be going into depth around each one as we progress through this book. It was with these steps that I saw myself go from four on-call shifts a week with just enough money to cover my essential expenses, but no energy to enjoy the rest, to choosing to work only fifteen days a month for myself, generating more than triple what I was earning in just thirty percent of the time. I saw my income streams multiply and my professional status grow to the point where I was invited to give talks in some of the most prestigious settings.

Now, this book is not intended to be about self-glorification, as I am still on my journey but, I very quickly realised that I had to share this knowledge.

From time to time I was still doing the odd locum hospital shifts to maintain the adrenaline rush, and every time I did, I found myself preaching my new discovery to other medics, nurses, surgeons and anybody around me. I was so excited by it and I wanted everyone to have a taste of it. Of course, over time I appreciated that not everyone was interested in what this strategy had to offer, but I became increasingly aware that many more than I had expected wanted to know. Herein lies the genesis of this book. I wanted to share exactly how I did it and how I began helping others do it so that all healthcare professionals could enjoy the fountain of opportunity.

You see, the original title of this book was 'The Modern Healthcare Professional' and only when I started writing it did I realise the title was incomplete. The title failed to convey a pivotal fact - I was never spending more than 8 hours, or a normal working day, each week planning and implementing the key steps! In fact, the other days of the week were simply the machine running, no need for heavy lifting.

I remember trying to convince an ENT consultant colleague of mine about my new discovery. I was eagerly telling her all about my journey and my intentions to help all healthcare professionals who were interested in enhancing their quality of life. With keen ears, she listened and responded, "These steps sound brilliant, but for people like me with the job and children, there is no time to put this into place". It was her response that reinforced the realisation that I was onto a winning formula that all of us could replicate. Committing 8 hours a week will bring you an improved quality of life within one year. That's all it takes.

And for those of you expecting a turnaround quicker than one year, yes you'll start to see an evolution before then, but do not expect any results that will be robust enough to last a lifetime; there is no such thing as overnight success – this is probably the closest thing to it.

Why Are Healthcare Professionals ("HCPs") Special?

You're probably wondering why I am so focused on healthcare professionals. Why is the strategy not applicable to everyone else everywhere? Is this just professional nepotism? Well unapologetically, that is part of the reason. Do you see any harm in it? I sure don't. It's about time that we looked out for each other as HCPs. Of course, anyone could take this methodology and apply it to a degree of success, but it won't yield as much mind-blowing results and that leads me to my next point.

As HCPs we are already experts, whether you're an ENT surgeon or theatre nurse. The moment you decide to pick a niche you enjoy or love, as long as it is even loosely connected to your professional field, your credibility is transferable. For example, even though any layman could research and figure out how the hair growth cycle works, a doctor in the field of cardiology will instantly have more credibility speaking on the same topic; simply because it is biological in nature. In a world where perceived experts have the greatest opportunities, it's ironic that the most credible people are actually making the least waves out there! The rest of the business world must literally celebrate that as a profession we are too busy to creatively monetise our knowledge and status. I didn't realise this until I took a moment to appreciate that being a doctor gave me huge credibility within my aesthetics niche. I then realised that the same thing goes for diet. Many doctors and nutritionists are enjoying being niche experts in an area not directly related to their day to day professional practice. You'll see this in many places – a professional qualification, if used correctly, is the ultimate advantage in establishing yourself as a leader in a niche. It was almost amusing to think that on a daily basis I was working with all these very highly credible people who had no idea how much value their opinion held in the community. This is the other reason I embarked on sharing my journey. I wanted us to gain some power back as a sector and share our inner expertise. In case you're thinking that this can only be relevant to doctors, just remember that we are only compared to each other when we occupy the same niche. Otherwise we are compared to the layman who actually can never carry your credibility in a niche related or loosely linked with your field of knowledge. You need to own that knowledge and throw away all notions of being an imposter!

Another reason that I knew it was crucial for me to share my experiences was because of my earlier point. We, as a group, are time poor. As such, many of the podcasts and audiobooks we listen to do not take into account night shifts, on-call shifts, erratic work patterns; all needing to be balanced with family and social commitments.

The point is, we are the group most likely to benefit from finding and exploiting the right niche but we are also the group with the least capacity to get out-of-work tasks done. When you add this to the fact that we have been highly selected, groomed and institutionalised you can see the struggle in breaking out of the status quo. I hope this book can help achieve that for you.

Some of you reading will have tried to create for yourselves a version of what I've described. More money, more time, etc. In fact, it might be the case for many of you who have an NHS job with some "side hustle". You see, I've come across many HCPs who have successfully set up a secondary income stream, but they've done this in an unscalable fashion, which means that they are so time poor they are unable to set up a foundation that will allow them to build further income streams which ought to allow them claim back their most valuable commodity - time. The big failures I often see are 'herd' mentality (which we all seem to be subject to at some point) and this means we occupy the same niches and so have to work very hard, sacrificing a lot of time to keep that secondary income flowing. Remember we don't just want more money; we want more time too. That is the way you need to be thinking if you want to improve your quality of life. Going through this system is designed to instil a foundation that will allow you to have more revenue, more satisfaction and more time. What is even more frustrating is that some of us try to free up our time by outsourcing to marketing companies and social media managers. I definitely agree that some of them are good but, with this method, you won't need to sacrifice a high proportion of your income and if you really want to outsource you will be able to direct your content managers in a way that won't lead to frustration. This was crucial for me, I needed to have control back in my life and only let people into places where I absolutely had no technical capacity to complete the task. Even then I was able to get exactly what I wanted from those relationships. Your content manager or SEO person has a technical skill but are not a strategist. You are the master of your own vision.

My final point on our unique healthcare family is that I don't expect my views to be popular. I'm not even sure the views would spread as easily as they should. You see, a few months into this strategy and you will begin to "see the light" and that isn't necessarily beneficial to the systems and institutions we are already part of. Well, that's what the misinformed may think! Here's the thing. It creates more time, more income, more career satisfaction and an overall better quality of life. It does not mean that you have to leave your current hospital or community role! In fact, the benefits I have seen, allows us to have a much healthier relationship with our main roles, and this means we work far better and give a better representation of ourselves. So, don't for one second think that you are being encouraged to leave the post you trained so hard to occupy. Let's face it; if we all did that we'd be in trouble. I would personally want HCPs to be energised, happy practitioners. That will soon be you.

The Right Mindset

Now, I'm not a psychologist nor am I here to teach you how to train your mind. However, I think until you get into the correct mindset this process simply won't work and I wanted to share with you the mindset I had to adopt to bring success.

Visualising the end

To me, this has always been the most important mental requirement in order to make my method or any other successful plans work. You need to have a vision. That vision can be anything you want it to be, whether it's spending more time with your family, moving into a dream home or being internationally recognised. For me it was and still is, being financially free by 40. I sat down and attached a value to that, and decided I needed to generate that passive income in order for it to happen. That guided my decision making and I accepted from that point onwards, that I can reassess what I wanted to achieve in my life. You see, a vision will frame your entire life and guide the decisions you make. Without it, your internal compass is likely to be easily swayed by external forces and you won't get to the finish line. I started this process with the end goal in mind and had it written on my wall, so I was constantly reminded of why I was taking an alternative path. You'll appreciate the value of this because we are always confronted by the norm and grow up thinking that being too different is a risk – you could end up on either extreme of the bell curve, right?! The truth, though, is that those mental limitations will also keep your life hovering around your perceived 'normal' and if you're reading this book then that is not where you want to be. So, visualise your goal, for now, and treat that as your personal mission statement. Oh, and if you're wondering why I've said, for now, it's because your "vision" will evolve once you've reached it; it's never the end!

Set realistic daily/ weekly tasks

This is life-changing. It sounds so simple, but most people do not do this. You're here because you want to change the dynamics of your professional life and that won't be handed to you. To make things worse, you're probably overworked and tired and using the little free time you have to read this book! So, with that in mind, we need to make your 8 hours as efficient as possible. Once you hit maximum efficiency, you'll go through the six steps at a blistering pace. The way I reached that point was to wake up every morning and set out my goals for the day, first thing. At times, I did this the night before. I created a rule where I would only seek to accomplish three tasks a day, and by tasks, I considered everything a task. Emails – a task, phone calls – a task, supporting Crystal Palace FC – a task etc. With this, I made sure I always completed my three tasks. I was never overstretched, and I became used to completing my to-do-list and it could co-exist alongside my regular job. And you see, after five days of three tasks a day, well, you can do the math. The point is you avoid the feeling of things piling up which is one of the biggest causes of procrastination. Another beautiful thing about this system I created is that I always wanted to have some type of mini win each day, and so I would be forced to prioritise which three tasks would give me the most satisfaction for the day if I completed them. Sometimes that was as simple as finding an email address! Again, I'm not some self-proclaimed mind coach, but this has worked for me and others I've shared this with. You want to keep that momentum. It's for that reason I suggest not condensing your 8 hours into one day. You'll likely lose momentum, start to procrastinate and become comfortable with not achieving the million tasks you laid out. Instead, consider stealing forty minutes here, or an hour there. It racks up and it works. Believe me, you'll rarely spend the entire eight hours a week if you're working effectively. Oh, and don't get me wrong, sometimes the greatest satisfaction is just by marking your tasks as complete.

The 'Now' mentality

One of the great skills I was able to garner from being temporarily part of the Silicone Roundabout community as a student (UK's Silicone Valley equivalent) was the ability to start things now. In that world, it felt like a race to get your ideas out, and sometimes it was, but what was useful was the absence of procrastination. There is an energy, or a spirit that accompanies just starting something. Or as Nike have coined "just do it". I think the main reason is that you break any doubt or fear that accompanies thinking a task is too huge. The truth is that even the biggest tasks in the world are a summation of loads of tiny accomplishments and completed tasks. For example, before writing my first book, the idea of a book seemed very daunting and completely out of my comfort zone. I spent far too long researching it and watching

YouTube videos and realised I hadn't actually got started after a couple of weeks in. So, I decided to put a hard stop one day, while sitting in The Hoxton Hotel, and just began writing the plan in detail. Once I started, I realised I was still breathing, and that day I wrote out my entire plan. The next day I began writing the book, deciding that the majority of my spare time would be spent doing this - 750 words per day - that was the goal. In reality, I enjoyed writing so much that I very often exceeded my goal and had to stop myself. The result was what seemed like such a daunting task was done twice as fast than I had expected and that was all down to the power of just starting. Truth is, most things aren't that bad once you break them down into manageable chunks. So, in case the message was lost, just start now. If something comes to you and you're on the train, look into it, or plan it while you're sitting there. Getting started will quickly provide you with useful time-saving insights that allow you to break the task down in the most manageable way.

The 'test, test, test' mentality

I want to give an honourable mention to the 'test test test' mentality. As healthcare professionals, we love a good old test. Yet, there is one test that we, like the majority of the world, don't particularly enjoy engaging in – testing our assumptions. This was the rate limiting step in my journey and once I was able to readjust my mindset to have awareness of my assumptions and test them; I saw some very amazing things happen. I'll give you guys an example. I subconsciously assumed that because of who I was or wasn't, there was no way I could cold message and build a relationship with the CEO of one of the largest worldwide luxury perfume brands. Being on my new journey of enlightenment I asked myself, why was it such a crazy idea? I had no answer, so, I messaged him on LinkedIn and months later he now sits as an advisor on my cosmetic product range. You see, we have to always test our assumptions about our services, our products and ourselves to really glide through this six-step process. Don't allow yourself to create your own cage of mental limitations. That's all I'll say on that point.

Right, so now you're in the appropriate state of mind for you to enhance your life in just 12 months and with just 8 hours a week. Let's get into the how...

Summary:

This six-step process is designed to give you a more fulfilled, flexible and financially rewarding life.

It only requires eight hours a week and the transformation takes one year. This way, you can do it alongside your work and social commitments.

The six steps are: find your niche, build your pitch, publish in your space, create a product/service, proliferate a consistent profile, collaborate.

As a healthcare professional you are a perceived expert. Therefore, you have an inbuilt advantage in the world of entrepreneurship. You are in a prime position to establish yourself as an expert within a particular field.

Three excellent mind frames to adopt include: visualising the end, set realistic daily/weekly goals, adopt a "now" mentality.

The "test test test" mentality is your prompt to challenge your assumptions at all times. Ask yourself, "How do I know?" when you find yourself coming to conclusions.

Step 1. Find Your Niche

Principle 1: Find yourself a micro-niche. That way your voice will be heard. Groups of people will look for you because you are offering something there isn't much of.

Principle 2: The more focused the niche, the more likely you are to have success.

Principle 3: You are a healthcare professional and so pick a niche that ties into health in some way. Otherwise pick a niche that is tied into your skill, whether a surgeon, psychiatrist or physio, however, it doesn't need to be what you do on a day to day basis.

So, we're finally at the point when we delve into the details of each step and kicking us off is the niche step. It probably would have been more appropriate to title this chapter 'your sub-niche' or 'your micro-niche'. One might argue that these terms are interchangeable. Practically, they both relate to a level more specific in its targeting than a regular niche. I will certainly go on to explain what these terms mean and most importantly what they mean to you. However, for those of you who just love knowledge in the form of books then one of the most trailblazing texts about the power of a niche is the 'Blue Ocean Strategy' by W. Chan Kim and Renée Mauborgne. This was the book that inspired my thinking and what I based many of my principles on. So, what is a niche? As an adjective it is: *denoting or relating to products, services, or interests that appeal to a small, specialized section of the population.* In simple speak, it is an area of interest that appeals to a specific group and not the general masses.

I'm going to take this moment just to remind you what your objective is here. Create multiple streams of income, create more time, and have increased recognition as an expert in your chosen area. So, with that in mind, the only way you can achieve those outcomes is to be the sort of person people want to hear, see, and give money too. You need fans. Okay, now that your mind is primed let's get back to niches.

In reality, almost everything we see in this world exists in a niche. It's why we don't buy our cars from Asda or our food from Apple (I just realised how odd that sounded). Because, most things already exist in a niche, being part of a niche doesn't really create any separation or distinction. Therefore, you'll be hard to discover and will inevitably have to work extra hard, spend extra money and time just to be a drop in a big ocean. The idea of the niche area is that you want to be the only person in your environment. You might have a few others, but you want to be a big fish in a smaller pond; contrary to common belief. Sometimes this pond might be overcrowded in another part of the world but relatively unexplored in your geographical region. This too represents a blue ocean opportunity giving you all the room in the world to operate because it's essentially only you. So, hopefully now you understand why being part of a niche is never enough and oftentimes you need to go one or two levels deeper.

"But Dr Uche, if you become so focused on a small target group you won't have any audience!" This is true if you focus, for example, on a disease where only one person in the world has it, but otherwise, for most things, there is a big enough audience out there for you. The key is to rewire your thinking. It only takes 1,000 people across the world to buy £1,000 worth of your products or services and you'll have brought in £1million. If you met a Youtuber with 1,000 subscribers, would you be blown away? Okay, maybe if you know the work it entails, but we all know and follow people with tens of thousands of people following them across many platforms. Personally, when I went into the non-surgical cosmetic industry, I thought I had found a sub niche; with the main niche being beauty. However, I learned that wasn't where I needed to stop. Contrary to the stories I had heard about doctors in aesthetics making loads of money, what I found was that I was offering the same service in the same way as so many. I found it hard to differentiate myself and I was actively looking for my clients. This meant that I was bearing a high customer acquisition cost and I was spending a lot of time and money attending many different advanced training courses looking for an edge. I also found that by putting out a lot of the same information as everyone else I was jumping from subtopic to subtopic while remaining incognito for any knowledge in any specific area. I spent six months building my online profile this way and as soon as I realised I was falling into a trap, I decided to stop and cleared my profile entirely with a view to starting again. It was in the coming months when I decided to focus on just under eyes and it was then that I realised that I was one of the few (if not the only) voices in that area. True to expectations, the benefits of having a micro-niche started to

materialise before my eyes. The first thing I noticed was that by making content that I enjoyed and staying focused, people began to look for me. Not just customers, but people who wanted me to work for them, people who wanted me to give talks, people who wanted to collaborate. I was no longer having to do the searching and I very quickly became the go-to person in the area. The ultimate proof of this was seeing my peers also recognise me as the go-to authority in the area. Remember what I said - blue ocean. You want to be the only (big) fish in your pond and while there may be only 1,000 people in the world who care about your topic, you will be one of the few persons, if not the only one, catering for their need. You will become the authority in the eyes of those people, and they will contribute to your growth far more than the fickle consumer with hundreds of options.

The next principle is a direct challenge to what most of us intuitively believe and with good reason. Most of the well-known, successful vendors that we buy from exist in a niche but seem to cover all bases. Just look at Apple, Amazon or Sainsbury's. Well, here's the thing that isn't common knowledge. Amazon started as an online bookstore. Apple started with only computers. Do you get my drift? Once you're an established brand, your fans will purchase almost anything from you. But the hard part is establishing that early group of supporters. The only way you catch them is by being something they haven't seen before and need, and so the idea of being more niche becomes rational.

Most interactions of exchange between people are based on trust; especially where money is involved. So you buy something assuming it will work or be of the quality you expect, and the other party takes your money trusting that it is not counterfeit nor will you attempt to rob them immediately afterwards. The point I am making is that we all buy based on trust and the more expert you are perceived to be the more people will trust you. Things start to become sticky when you have many 'experts' in the same arena and this is why you want to be the lone expert where possible. I can imagine some of you saying, "well, you're never alone", that is true, but by the law of Google, if you look for something and can't really find it on the first page then you're alone. So actually, the logic follows, be as niche as you can be without dwindling down your target market to zero; you'll quickly become an influencer in the space, develop supporters and fans who have been looking for what you now offer (be that feeling, service or product) and they will spread the word for you. On the flip side you don't want to be so niche nobody wants to hear what you have to say, but in my experience, that's hard to do so I suggest not worrying about it too much.

Now, just to drive the point home that the more niche you are the likelier you are to achieve success, consider this scenario. Let's say you want to spend £200 on an educational toy for your 2-year-old child. Which of these places are you most likely to look for and purchase such a toy from?

a) Tesco Superstore

b) Toys R' Us

c) Lego for children under 6 years old

d) Early Learning Centre

Hopefully, like me, you went for option D. As you can see the options became progressively more niche and so too did your affinity to spend. Now imagine you took this even further. Your child is 2 years old and you wanted something educational around languages?

e) Early Learning Centre

f) Language play centre for children

g) The early language play centre for advanced pre-school children

Do you see my point? It is always more compelling to be more niche because motivated consumers (the ones you want) always have a need and they would want someone who can fulfil that need. The more general you are the more you cater to unmotivated, fickle consumers who will flit around and never aid your growth as they are inundated with loads of choices.

Did you also notice something else? £200 for a toy is quite a lot of money to spend, but it seems far more expensive to spend that in Tesco than it does in The Early Language Play Centre for Advanced Pre-School Children (this is not a real store, by the way, at least I don't think so). The reason for this is simple. As a perceived expert you instantly overcome price resistance. This means that market prices are always being driven down by the lowest price and in order to escape the price comparison you have to be seen as an expert in what you do; a cut above the rest if you like. Of course, the easiest way to achieve this is to be super niche as you will be in a blue ocean (remember that term) from the beginning and have a chance to make yourself the Authority. As a result, people will pay whatever you say because they will believe you are the Authority in that micro-niche and that comes with a sense of status. On the other hand, people will pay whatever you ask, simply because there isn't any other comparison out there!

Therefore, the take-home message for this principle is to try to be as niche as you can. Think about the exact customer/client you want to serve and what they are looking for. That will guide you to establishing your niche, bringing us on to the next point quite nicely - how are you going to pick yours?

Well, for those of you who are not aware, I have been using these six steps to provide one to one consultations with healthcare professionals. However, when I first tested my principle and began the journey of knowing how applicable it was outside of me; my very first client was actually not in healthcare at all. It was a property investor who asked me how to help her find her niche brand. To help her find her niche, we created a small table with all the things that made her (the stuff people would point out) on the x-axis and all of her passions and interests on the y-axis. In the end, it looked something like this:

	Female	Nigerian	Mixed	Dutch	Cambridge degree	Tall	Under 30	Property Investor	Professional Investor	City worker	Large Organisation employee	No Children	Single	Full time Employee
Property														
Social mobility														
Property rejuvenation														
Female Empowerment														
Fitness														
Investing														
Financial Literacy														

From this we were able to generate multiple micro-niches, identifying which ones she liked best. Axis X represented all the areas that would allow her to easily access expert status as she was already either that thing or had previously done that thing. The Y-axis represented her interests and passions and now it was about putting the two together. For example: "Helping full-time employees of large organisations to invest in underdeveloped areas through property". Or here's another one, "coaching females under 30 in full-time employment on becoming financially free through investment in HMOs (homes with multiple occupancies)". So, this is one method to generate ideas for your micro-niche that will keep you relatively close to your area of expertise.

As healthcare professionals it's probably even easier than this to pick a niche. You can tie almost anything in this world back to health (physical and mental), fitness and safety. I'm not quite sure of an area in this world where a healthcare professional cannot express an interest and the most beautiful thing about all of this is that because you have this credibility you don't necessarily need to be focusing on the same thing in both your side hustle and main hustle. Of course, it helps even more if the two align, but most untapped niches do not have degree or certificate entry requirements attached to them. The position of expert is often awarded to the most dedicated person who is willing to share their knowledge and being a healthcare professional, if you are relating a topic back to health, fitness or safety then it is assumed that your skills are transferable. As I said, it certainly helps when there is alignment between your professional calling and your passion because it creates an even higher barrier for competitors who may wish to seek to take your shine; but it is not make or break if they do not align. You see, credibility like all things, has different levels. I became the Cosmetic Eye doctor without ever having been an Oculoplastic Surgeon. I didn't need specialist training to learn what I had learned and do what I did, but would it make it even better if I was an oculoplastic surgeon? I believe so. Would it have made it better if I was a Cardio thoracic surgeon? No. And we see this all the time, while it can help to align your passion and work, the truth is; how trustworthy you are within one of the broader sectors (in this case health, fitness, beauty, safety) is the real determinant of what you can and cannot do. Have you heard of Dr Pimple Popper? I'm not sure how much pimple popping our dermatology friends actually do, but it didn't stop her. Or what about the food medic with over 400K followers on Instagram? She never did any speciality training nor was she a nutritionist before establishing herself. Now of course, not all of you will be medical doctors, and yes, being a doctor does afford a great degree of flexibility, but as a healthcare professional you have far more flexibility than the layman. Find your niche, then micro-niche, and start asserting yourself as an expert in that area. If it is something that you are already passionate about then you probably have far more knowledge than everyone else and people want to hear or experience it!

Summary:

Finding a micro-niche is far more beneficial to your growth than operating within a wider niche.

Expert status and organic growth are easier to achieve within a micro-niche.

Ideally, pick a health related area that you are passionate about, then pick a group of people who you can help within that area. This is the guide to finding your micro-niche.

Exercise:

Create yourself a table of your skills and experience (x-axis) and passions (y-axis). Can you see where two of them can combine to create a micro-niche for you?

Step 2. Build Your Pitch

Principle 1: A pitch serves as your introduction to all the people who meet you. It's the foundation of all you do or say from here on. It's your new identity.

Principle 2: You should be able to deliver your pitch within 1 minute.

Principle 3: A strong pitch should always lead to people asking questions to know more about HOW you do what you do.

Having found your micro-niche, you now need a way to communicate it with the world in a short and snappy way. This is where your pitch comes in. This stage really shouldn't be taken lightly because it is the difference between your growth happening quickly or slowly. Why do I say that? Well, your pitch is the aspect of your business you'll be confronted with the most. Having a true understanding of your pitch allows you to frame all the future steps and think about exactly what it is your clients and followers want.

So, what do you do for a living? A very common question, right? Or how about, {enter description/bio} on a social media platform like Instagram or LinkedIn, or an 'about' section on a website, or the first 10 words of your site on a Google search. You see, almost everywhere you turn the first thing people want to hear is your pitch and attention spans are not very long, so you only have a short time or a few characters to make an impression. It's a very hard skill and the vast majority of people never have to think about it and so say things that could never drive business or growth in their prospective field. Common mistakes at this stage include saying something that's vague, full of technical jargon, or not unique. By having discovered your micro-niche you should already be able to get around the vagueness issue. Nobody is interested in anything vague because people surfing the web or meeting for the first time are prepared to offer their attention to the highest bidder, and so you have to grab their attention and show them you might be exactly what they are looking for. Part of not losing the interest of listeners or readers in your pitch is staying straight to the point in a short time span, but also in a language that they will understand. Jargon alienates people and leaves them seeking out things that they do understand. As per being unique, you will already have accomplished that because you have found a micro-niche where you fit in.

In order to break down a strong pitch, we are going to analyse and compare a variety of pitches and as a reader you can decide which one you think is better. Now, even though I will be highlighting the differences between pitches, try and stay ahead of the game by coming to your own decisions about the quality of the pitches. Then see if you will be able to improve anything to make the pitch more compelling. Remember, your pitch is like your mission statement and will serve as the core for all you say or do around your personal brand from here on in.

Niche: Strategy and branding for HCPs

Weak pitch: I help healthcare professionals make more money.

Strong pitch: I help healthcare professionals find an expert niche and expand it so they can generate multiple streams of passive and active income. I guarantee this with just eight hours a week.

Analysis: Let's start with the obvious. Pitch number 1, the weak pitch, was unbelievably vague and gave no actual insight into what the subject does. Can you imagine meeting this person at a party or seeing this on a LinkedIn profile? It's not memorable, conveys no sense of expert status, and though you may be intrigued, you may be scared that you're about to have a recruiter pitch to you. One good point, however, is that it is short and to the point and still is somewhat niche, and as a result, raises some level of intrigue. Imagine if it said "I help people make more money" you'd have no interest as you've probably heard that one million times.

Pitch number 2, the strong pitch on the other hand, goes into a fair amount of detail while still being delivered in under one minute and in just two sentences. By going into some detail about how they help HCPs make added streams of income, the natural intrigue is to find out how this is done in just eight hours per week. It's far more compelling and is more likely to have you asking for a website or content to watch; you want to know more about these claims. Further to this, pitch 2 also creates a guide as to how you can structure your business. It sets clear principles about the aim to create an active and passive income, it has a focus on expert niches, and it creates strategies that won't demand more than 8 hours per week from those following it.

Niche: Nonsurgical cosmetics for under eyes

Weak pitch: I'm an aesthetics doctor working on under eyes.

Strong pitch: I'm the non-surgical cosmetic doctor people come to see when they look tired and they've tried everything within their power to correct it and failed. I make them look more refreshed without surgery.

Analysis: I want you to put yourself in the position of a patient and you come across two campaigns with either of the above messages. Which one are you going to call first? Hopefully, you said the second pitch. Why don't you at this point make a note, mental or physical, of all the reasons why you chose the second pitch.

Okay, so you've made the list. Here's my breakdown. Pitch number one once again is niche and does convey some degree of expert status. However, it still leaves you a little confused and doesn't appeal to the differing crowds within cosmetics. Some may see this and instantly assume the subject is a plastic surgeon and therefore want to stay away as they're not interested in surgery. Its vagueness leaves the listener or reader generating many questions and the result of that is a feeling of angst followed by avoidance. People don't want to be confused or overwhelmed with questions trying to figure out if you can even help them. When compared to the second pitch you can see pitch two's strengths instantly. Firstly, it cleverly calls to a group of people within the cosmetic herd; 'people who look tired'. This creates an instant feeling of belonging, understanding, and assurance for all those who have been battling this issue. It also conveys expert status by elevating the subject's skills above interventions that potential customers could complete at home; the practitioner is clearly advanced. Lastly, after setting up the listener by showing an understanding of the issues at hand, the pitch then goes on to shed light on what the subject does and how they do it- 'more refreshed but without surgery'. It leaves just enough for readers/listeners to want to see more about how this is achieved.

Niche: Hair loss conditions in young women

Weak pitch: I specialise in hair loss in young people.

Strong pitch: I specialise in diagnosing and treating hair loss conditions in young women, particularly those forty and under. My methods allow women to remedy their hair loss at home and without the need for a hair transplant.

Analysis: Once again the level of detail in the strong pitch allows your audience to identify themselves without confusion, and a by-product of that is a presumed expert status. The weak pitch doesn't give any insight into who 'young people' are. That could be 5-year olds or 40-year olds. And, while it does suggest an expert niche because it is topic-specific, the feeling of "I must be getting the best here" isn't really aroused. It's more of an "I'll see who else offers the same thing" feeling. Contrastingly, the second pitch creates a focus and even gives insight into the 'how'. This not only makes you seek more information, but it also lulls you into a heightened sense of security. Imagine if you were a 32-year-old woman with traction alopecia. You've seen multiple Google adverts for Trichologists, but then you come across this advert. Your attention will be instantly grabbed, and you'll probably be sold from the start. As humans, most of our decisions to buy are emotional and we then use rationale to justify those decisions. That decision-making process happens in seconds and then it's a case of justifying our initial decision.

Niche: Dietary supplements for workers

Weak pitch: I review the best dietary supplements for people who work in the services sector. The issue I target in particular is fatigue and my reviews go into depth about the bioavailability and efficacy of these supplements. By the end of my analysis I recommend which supplements are best. My typical audience are workers that are on their feet for long periods of time.

Strong pitch: Many people who work in jobs that require them to be on their feet for long periods of time suffer from fatigue; this makes doing their job even harder. I discover, review and recommend the best supplements for such people, to help boost energy levels naturally.

Analysis: Okay, so this was a slightly different scenario. What are your initial thoughts? Here you can see what happens when you don't keep things concise. Not only are you having to read 3 sentences before you know whether or not you belong to the target group, but it also has technical jargon like 'bioavailability'. This is a sure-fire way to lose your audience. Keeping the language simple and using examples to explain complicated concepts is key to engaging with your audience. Data has shown that during U.S presidential elections, the winning candidate often delivered speeches at a lower academic speaking grade than those who lost (think Trump, think Bush). Keep it simple, but also keep it brief! Our attention spans are not that long, so avoid a long, drawn-out pitch.

Now, in truth, there were quite a few concepts to communicate in this last pitch. The idea of what the supplements help with, who they're for and the subject's role in this dynamic. In order to get this all across and keep it engaging, a good tactic is storytelling. If you frame your pitch as a story that people can relate to this will be far more engaging as people want to hear the climax. In the strong pitch, you can see that the focus is on the people being helped and not the subject or what the subject can offer. Framing it this way keeps interest as the audience wants to know where you fit in. The second sentence in the pitch then introduces the subject; by having a specific focus and highlighting the 'how', instant expert status is assumed. The audience will already believe the subject is an authority in the space.

Hopefully, by now you have a good idea about how to construct a strong pitch. Remember our 3 principles:

Principle 1: A pitch serves as your introduction to all prospective clients/customers who meet you. It's the foundation of all you do or say from here on. It's your new identity.

Principle 2: You should be able to deliver your pitch in 1 minute, so it should be short and snappy.

Principle 3: A good pitch should always lead to people asking questions to know more about HOW you do what you do.

By using the illustrative scenarios below, you can identify a template that you can use to build your own pitch. Remember, the steps are completed sequentially, so by the time you think about your pitch you should have picked and validated your expert niche.

The fun really kicks in when you have to adapt your pitch for platforms that only give you a few words as a limit. For example, bios on your Instagram page or LinkedIn profile may only be a handful of words and you have to make them count. I refer to this as 'pitch condensing', and it is pretty straight forward when you take into account the three principles.

Your condensed pitch should identify your audience and highlight your expertise. Admittedly, it's much harder to have the same impact in such a few words but, incorporate those two key elements and you'll signpost the audience towards delving deeper.

Illustrative Scenario 1

Strong pitch: I'm the non-surgical cosmetic doctor people come to see when they look tired and they've tried everything within their power to correct it but failed. I make them look more refreshed without surgery.

Condensed version: non-surgical solutions to tired looking eyes

Illustrative Scenario 2

Strong pitch: I specialise in diagnosing and treating hair loss conditions in young women, particularly those forty and under. My methods allow women to remedy their hair loss at home and without the need for a hair transplant.

Condensed version: Home remedies for hair loss in women under 40.

Illustrative Scenario 3

Strong pitch: I help healthcare professionals find an expert niche and expand it so they can generate multiple streams of passive and active income. I guarantee this with just eight hours a week.

Condensed version: Attention Healthcare Professionals! Click to exploit your expertise for more money and time.

That's it for building your pitch. Throughout this chapter, you should have been prompted to think about how you will construct your pitch around your expert niche. Already have it done? Great, stick it on your wall so that you can remind yourself of exactly what direction to take with your future steps. And, lastly, do not be afraid to refine and improve your pitch. Every step of this process can be revisited and refined; it won't take you backward unless you completely overhaul your expert niche.

Summary:

Once you have found your niche, in step one, creating a pitch is the next step.

A strong pitch is your chance to grab your audience's attention.

Keep the pitch short and concise but avoid being too vague and ensure there is enough detail to avoid confusion of your audience.

Technical jargon has no place in a pitch.

Exercise:

You have your niche now. Create a pitch that you can deliver within one minute and try it out on friends and family. See what they think.

Once you have written your pitch and you have learned it by heart, progress to creating a 'condensed pitch' you can use where word limits are a restriction.

For both options; create multiple options and see which ones get the best response. Think about why that is.

Step 3. Publish In Your Space

The publishing stage is all about your "trust score". This is analogous to a credit rating whereby you are credit-scored. Now, I'm sure many of you understand how credit-scoring works, however, I'll quickly recap in a non-technical way. So, you want to have access to credit (the ability to borrow money), but the only way lenders can really know that you are credit-worthy is via this thing called a credit score. You can build your creditworthiness only by having a credit history, but some things you do have a bigger impact on building your score than others. The aim of the game is to get to the perfect 999 and then you have the complete trust of lenders and they will basically lend you whatever you want. Publishing in the world of personal branding works in exactly the same way. You prove yourself by sharing your knowledge and you will work up to this perfect trust score where the majority of your target audience will be loyal fans. And even though there are many ways to get to that perfect trust score the different methods weigh differently. Hopefully, this analogy makes sense to you and you can appreciate the importance of publishing.

The question now is, "What is actually meant by publishing?" Quite simply, this is where you get your ideas, expertise, and commentaries out to the public. Publishing can come in many forms: digital magazines, print magazines, books, animated videos, podcasts and the list continues. It's all about disseminating your expert knowledge and opinions. I have personally found this to be the most creative part of the six-step process and it really allows you to distinguish yourself.

As previously mentioned, not all forms of publishing are made equal. What does that mean? Well, writing and publishing a book has far more weight than an Instagram story post or even most forms of online articles. When you're deciding on how you want to publish your thoughts remember that certain forms of publishing build trust more than others. There are, however, some exceptions to this rule. For example, having a podcast or video series (normally not as impactful as a book) with famous celebrities is a form of publication that may exceed releasing a book that didn't attract much fanfare. It is also important that when deciding on the platform to publish you must keep in mind your strengths, as it's always a good idea to play to your greatest attributes.

With all this being said, I will break down the multiple forms of publishing and how they can help you.

Online Articles

This is tried and tested and remains one of the original ways to publish and build your credibility. I learned very quickly not to underestimate how much people read. I know it's easy to assume otherwise in this age of YouTube and Instagram, but people still refer to online articles that they find via Google searches as their first port of call when looking for information. As long as Google search is a thing, online articles will always have their place. Furthermore, the reason I distinguish online articles from other articles, in general, is that they offer so much more than meets the eye. Yes, people will read your articles, perhaps enjoy the content and that in itself builds your credibility. However, articles online can create backlinks in the world of the web which is a key part of search engine optimisation. For those of you unfamiliar with this term; without trying to oversimplify it, it is the process of making yourself more visible on Google searches. As such, if you have online articles or blogs connected to your website then you are better placed to be found organically. People will share and reference your work far more readily.

Another major advantage of publishing online articles is that it is far easier to get into some of the most prestigious magazines and journals via their digital platform than one would their print platform. I know, I know, we all dream of seeing our names in a hard copy of Time magazine or the Evening Standard, but for the most part, these media groups have far more digital traffic. Now, don't get me wrong, I'm not purporting that being in the online version of Time magazine is better than the print copy – this is mainly because we tend to browse print magazines, but look for specifics online so the interaction is different. However, if it's easier to get featured online and you still get to add to your CV "featured in Time Magazine"; just do it.

Writing online articles and blogs need not be complicated either. As HCPs we tend to always think scientifically, which is fine, but sometimes your audience just wants your opinion. As a result, the content of the article you write should take on whatever form of your choosing. People want to hear what you have to say whether it's laced with facts or just a rant. Also, I often get asked about the lengths of these pieces. I'm no writing pro but the truth is that depending on your expert niche, the nature of the article and your audience, you'll need to adjust the length of the read accordingly. I hardly wrote articles above 500 words, but if your expert niche is quite scientific or a generally geekier area then more in-depth pieces are more likely to be better appreciated.

As far as trust scores go, online articles definitely are a must and go a long way to boosting your credibility. This is especially true if you can be featured in the big magazines or journals that your audience read. Bear in mind that content shared among your peers may be good for your ego and peer recognition, but if your audience does not read the BMJ and instead read Women's Health, then it's clear where you should be prioritising your efforts.

Books

Books have always been and always will be one of the highest impact ways of building your credibility in a field. Let's face it, writing a book isn't just something people do every day. Books communicate true expert command over a topic, instantly pitch you as an authority and speak to your dedication to an area. You can probably tell that I really love the idea of writing a book! It was one of the things that propelled my position within my expert niche and yielded so many benefits afterwards which we will go into now.

Firstly, a book will provide clarity for you on your chosen expert niche. Yes, believe it or not writing a book may have more benefit to your learning than even your intended audience. It will help you organise your thoughts and your message and also allow you to pinpoint your knowledge gaps – you want to make sure your book is clear and conveys the message you intend.

Secondly, from writing one book you create a 'script' for all future articles, videos, podcasts; it's incredible! I think of it like this: your pitch is the movie title, the book is the script, your articles, videos, and podcasts are your trailers. Once you have the script you can make all the trailers. The way this works is that often one chapter from your book will be the equivalent of one or two articles, one podcast episode, one online video and so on.

Thirdly, there is very little that trumps calling yourself an author. Off the top of my head, only a best-selling author sounds better. The beautiful thing as well is that you don't need your book to be a bestseller. It's the ultimate business card, the ultimate gift to your audience and accessory on your desk. It screams "expert" more than most things. Furthermore, getting a book out there is not as difficult as many think. With Amazon self-publishing services, you don't need to have an agent or be signed to a publishing company to have your book produced in paperback and digital copy.

Lastly, you'll be in the company of celebrities and other recognised figures as having purchasable written content on Amazon. This will massively strengthen your personal brand; which is useful if you ever seek outside investment for a future venture.

To be quite honest, there are probably way more reasons writing a book is just such a great way to go when publishing in your area. I must leave those reasons to become apparent to you once you've completed this part of your journey.

Now, what about the Elephant in the room? How the hell do you even go about writing a book? The answer is simple. Planning. Fallacy number one is that your book has to be written with the skill of JK Rowling and be five hundred pages long. It can be as long or short as you want, and your style of writing will be your style. This is your expert niche, so you have the knowledge in your head. You've spent ages fascinated, researching and learning about this topic and you can share that in fifty or five hundred pages; it's up to you. Also, the book style can take on any form. My first release was a '50 tips and tricks' book whereas you may choose to demonstrate your knowledge through a fictional story or a picture book; similar to what Rihanna released. The point is that your book can take on whatever format you want.

Once it's clear in your head what you want to write about then get to planning it out whether that be in an excel spreadsheet (my preferred method) or on your phone notes. The real key is to have clarity on the chapters and the message each chapter will convey. After that you'll edit and change as you go. Remember to keep these two pieces of advice in mind: i) set yourself a daily goal of 500-1,000 words to be written every day at a time that you can consistently replicate; ii) get started! Don't delay too much or get too bogged down in the title or planning. Writing a book is strange in that once you start you realise it's a very therapeutic process and is very hard to stop. You'll love it!

Podcasts

In the growing age of podcasts, you have a ready-made way to establish authority and credibility. And one of the great advantages of podcasts is the networking opportunity it provides. How so? Podcasts can take two different forms. The first form can be focused on you or your team, discussing particular topics. While this is a great way to showcase your knowledge or develop a cool debate format, it doesn't present the same network effect as the second popular type of podcast – interviews. By interviewing people with an opinion in your field, you not only lighten the demand on you for knowledge, but it gives people a different voice and draws in the audience of the interviewee. This is a very effective way to grow your audience without having to even budget for marketing. The interviewee will absolutely want their audience to see their content and as such, will be proactive in promoting. A podcast with an interview format very quickly becomes your chance to network with other thought leaders around your expert niche. People are always looking to talk about their stories and opinions, and this creates a great excuse to have a chance to sit down with people you may ordinarily struggle to meet. However, take note, getting these sit-down interviews comes by having a strong pitch.

Consider a podcast as one of your tools of gaining trust and keeping your publishing fresh. It may not have the same credibility score as writing a book, but over multiple episodes, you may have the same, and possibly more, trust from demonstrating status within your field. It is also worth noting that the idea of a podcast seemed like a very long and technically challenging process to me. However, after having been an interviewee on an associate's podcast, I was privileged enough to see the entire process and it was surprisingly easy with very little cost. Don't allow your assumptions to stop you from completing a simple Google search to determine what it would take for you to launch your own podcast.

Print Magazines / Newspapers

There are few prouder moments than at opening a recognised magazine or newspaper to find an article from you or about you. My first feature was in Aesthetic Medicine magazine in 2018 and it was certainly a moment of great pride for me. However, besides the great sense of achievement I felt on the day, something else happened. I received unexpected WhatsApp messages from friends and associates, with pictures of my article. You see, that is the reason why print magazines and newspapers are a big deal in the game of credibility. They still carry a sense of allure and prestige when compared to their online counterparts and, as previously mentioned, people will tend to browse magazines and newspapers and therefore are more likely to stumble across your content when compared to the specific search nature of online consumption. Now, whether or not your article is seen, it is more about your reach than your credibility, but it still stands to reason that as your content spreads so too does your trustworthiness and credibility.

Informational videos

These have proven to be one of my favourite and most reliable ways of building credibility (and also incredibly enjoyable if you like the camera). We are in the age of videos. Society has progressed from radio to television and now the YouTube generation; consuming short on-demand videos. So, it stands to reason that in order to get a piece of this pie you should also be making engaging short videos. Who doesn't love to speak about what they do or know? Take advantage of this method to bring information to your audience, but with several other benefits that extend beyond some of the other methods of publishing.

While it is possible to express your personality through writing, few other mediums can capture your nuances the same way as making videos. As people become drawn to your personality and charisma, they will add an attached value to your opinions and build trust for you.

Another reason that you should invest time in publishing via informational videos is that they allow you to easily share your content among many social media platforms with the work it takes to make a single video. You don't get the same benefit from writing online articles for example. Besides giving you immediate satisfaction from seeing your content liked, when your content is shared it builds additional trust and credibility as others share your work on your behalf. It acts as though people are vouching for you.

The downside of these informational videos is that they may cost quite a bit to have them made to an effectively appropriate standard, but they are certainly a good investment and often create a "celebrity" type feel to your brand which in turn increases your trust score.

Okay, so at this point, we've had a brief look at some of the most popular and effective ways to publish your knowledge. In my experience, many associate this stage of the process with the pains of writing university dissertations. If you take that approach, you'll never be motivated to do it. Take it from me, as someone who hated writing as part of my academic studies, when you produce content that can showcase a topic you are knowledgeable and passionate about, it's an enthralling process. By creating deadlines and setting manageable goals you can also produce a library of publishable content that could take months before you have released it all. It's a step that can happen anytime: on the commute, on a lunch break, with a glass of wine. Once you've begun publishing your knowledge, you'll be ready for the next stage; the money stage.

Summary

You've now identified your expert area and have the attention of others. Proving your expertise is the next step of the process.

Publishing is all about sharing your expertise and opinion with the general public.

By publishing content of different forms and on different platforms you quickly build your 'trust score' and progress towards people paying for your expertise.

Not all methods of publishing carry the same weight.

Popular publishing methods include online articles, books, podcasts, print magazines and informational videos.

Exercise:

Pick one of these methods of publishing and plan your first piece of content. Afterwards, look into the ways in which you can disseminate it.

Step 4: Create A Product / Service

At this point you have identified your expert niche and built an engaging pitch. You've successfully elicited interest in you and what you know. So, naturally, people want to know more about your micro-niche. They check you out on Google and see you have a book, articles, and some very engaging YouTube content. Wow. "You're the real deal", they're thinking, and exactly the person they have been looking for all this time. In the excitement they spread your name among others who they know would be well served by what you preach. As the audience grows and their trust in you hits new heights, they long to experience one of your services or products because they believe in you. They are not interested in the money they'd have to spend because you're the expert in an area devoid of competing professionals. What are you then going to offer?

Yes, this is the point you start adding additional streams of income to your day job. The part that begins to impact on your bank account and also the point you start to believe that maybe your life could be different from anything you had previously imagined. Now, the point of this chapter is not about telling you what you should do or offer because obviously, I have no idea what you will be doing. However, I do intend for this chapter to help you appreciate where many people go wrong.

To give some historical context, this chapter was written at the time of COVID-19 or Coronavirus; the world's biggest viral pandemic outbreak since the Spanish Flu of 1918. To be more specific, this chapter was written in the middle of a government enforced lockdown in London, designed to forcibly limit the movement and commerce of people to control the spread of this airborne virus. The impact of these government measures meant a massive loss of income for many. Legions of healthcare professionals saw their private practices and services close down indefinitely with no clear alternative source of income. Of course, for some, such as doctors and nurses, going back to support the NHS during the crisis provided a focus away from their private businesses and created a new purpose. However, for some healthcare professionals who were not necessarily contributing to the frontline during the crisis, the mental impact of lost income was in line with the general population. Why have I mentioned this? Well, at the time of writing this book, online businesses had witnessed a massive upward surge; a clear demonstration of the principle I had been enunciating for well over one year now. As healthcare professionals with aspirations to have autonomy, it's crucial to have more than one income stream, but it is even more crucial that the sources of those income streams are diversified in a similar way to a smartly constructed investment portfolio. What do I mean by that? Physical vs online. The trick is to turn your expertise into a service that can be given in person, but also online, and a product that can be sold physically and online. That might seem quite tricky to do, but actually it's quite straightforward. We'll dip into this concept more, but before we do, I also want you to have clarity on the following terms; active income versus passive income. Remember one of the key outcomes of this process is to create for you more time and so we need to be passive income heavy!

What is active income vs passive income? I'm sure you are familiar with these terms and so I won't dwell on them, but to put it simply, active income is the income you generate that is dependent on trading a unit of time for a sum of money. An example of this is when you go to work. You give up ten hours a day and in return you get paid. Discounting sick pay; if you do not go to work then you won't make the money. If you don't turn up for your clients then you won't be paid; it's the same thing. Passive income, on the other hand, is money you generate without having to exchange a unit of time. For those of you who are landlords, you will be experiencing the joys of passive income now. From a business perspective, if you sell toothpaste online it can sell around the world at any time and doesn't require your time for each sale. This is a passive income.

PHYSICAL   ONLINE

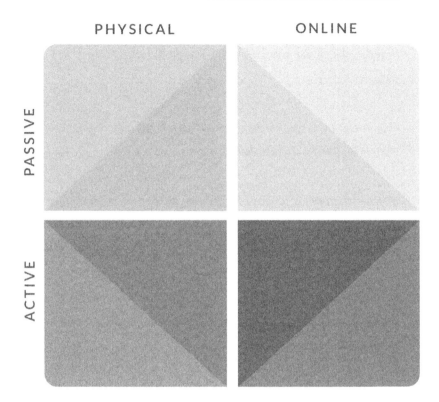

PASSIVE

ACTIVE

Thinking of your income in the following quadrants will allow you to identify where you're lacking and build more diverse income streams.

Now, let's see how you can combine the concepts of active and passive incomes with physical and online businesses.

Expert niche: A dentist who focuses on structural cosmetic teeth enhancements for professional boxers with a higher damage risk.

Primary work and interest: Clinic work using a variety of methods to improve the straightness of teeth for professional boxers and UFC fighters.

Income stream 1 (the main hustle / day job): Regular dental clinic where all dental services are provided.

Income stream 2: A service-based clinic, focused on straightening the teeth of boxers. The dentist has a patient list here and therefore has an active income in the physical form.

Income stream 3: Hires another dentist to provide the same niche service on a commission basis. This represents a passive income in the physical form.

Income Stream 4: Gives in-person training to other dentists who want to learn teeth straightening in challenging groups of patients. This is an active income in the physical form.

Income stream 5: Provides the same training as in stream 4, but this time online and for a reduced price. This represents a passive income and online.

Income stream 6: The dentist creates a novel gum shield and sells this to online retailers and sells directly to consumers. This represents a passive income online.

Income stream 7: This same product sells to physical shops, such as Sports Direct, and also out of other dental clinics. This represents a passive income in the physical form.

Wow. Even when I write this out it still surprises me. This dentist now has seven streams of income, six in addition to their regular job and that is off the back of one concept, one expert niche. This is the beauty of productising your knowledge. Where some HCPs go wrong, even the entrepreneurial ones, is that they get to income stream two or three and think it stops there. You see the issue is not that three income streams are not sufficient to dramatically change your life; but it's the combination that's the issue. Yes, having all your income in the physical form means you are highly exposed to things that can affect sales in the physical form. Regional regulation changes, storm damage, construction works, people being sick or underperforming, higher building rental costs and unforeseen emergencies like the Coronavirus pandemic. Of course, online businesses have their own concerns as well, but the point of this is to make you think about how you can create something you can sell online as well as in the physical form. The other part of this equation is having a product compared to a service. If you truly develop your expert niche, then there should be a product in there that you can produce to compliment your service. If you are a physio who performs spinal realignment, having an accompanying home product would have seen you make huge gains during the Coronavirus crisis; offsetting any loss on the service side. There is a product in all of us. Sometimes it's less obvious than at other times, but I'm yet to meet the expert who cannot offer a complimentary product. Furthermore, creating a product is often far less complicated than most things and oftentimes it is as easy as rebranding a white-label or template product that already exists. Newsflash! This is what the majority of the large companies do. I'll give you another example of how this works using myself.

Expert niche: non-surgical enhancement of the undereye area to hide or remove bags and dark circles.

Income stream 1: The Cosmetic Eye Clinic. A list of patients requiring my service. This represents an active income in the physical form

Income stream 2: Hire a second aesthetic practitioner in the Cosmetic Eye Clinic to work on a commission basis. This represents a passive income in the physical form.

Income stream 3: An in-person teaching course covering the techniques used in my daily practice. This represents an active income in the physical form.

Income stream 4: An online teaching video that covers all the same techniques and learning points as the in-person course. This represents a passive income in the online form.

Income stream 5: Reviewing products from eye companies producing serums for puffiness and lines around the eyes. This represents a passive income in the online form as products sold via affiliate marketing generate an income. You see affiliate marketing every time you see people selling a product and attaching their personal discount code. The company advertised turns the subject into a sales rep and in return the subject is paid commission. It's very effective if you have a highly engaged followership and you believe in what you are advertising.

Income stream 6: 'Eye Magic by Dr Uche', a racially inclusive under eye cream targeted at brightening dark circles, with formulations specific to skin colour and type. Online and physical retail stores. This represents passive income both in the physical and online form.

I've quickly drawn this up to demonstrate the point, but you could potentially add in talks, sponsorships for podcasts or YouTube channels, and even sales from published material such as a book (for some of you a book could be your product if it is something like a recipe book or teaching manual). The options are far more extensive than most of us, including me, ever truly appreciate. Once you lay out these streams in front of you, they also act as a very motivating list of goals. And, to reiterate, creating a product is not something you should be afraid of. It seemed daunting to me when I embarked on creating a luxury eye cream for dark circles, but after completing my research I quickly realised how many avenues there were for accomplishing this goal without compromising my vision and still for less than £10,000. I advise that the best way is to start small – get a taste for this new world.

Okay, so the take-home message from this chapter is to think about the ways you can turn your expert niche into a service and a product and then take it a step further by thinking about your active flow versus your passive flow. Once you have established the ways of diversifying your income your final challenge is to have an equal split of streams online and in the physical form. Don't get too bogged down with having equal revenue from both streams as that can be distracting. After you've completed the steps, you can then focus on that after your first year of owning your expert niche.

Summary

In this step you are monetising the expert status you have developed in the publishing stage.

By creating a product or service you can monetise your expertise within your micro-niche.

Ensuring that you have as many, if not more, passive streams of income compared to active streams of income, is the way to become time richer.

The COVID-19 crisis demonstrated to us all how crucial it is to have a strong online component to your income streams.

Exercise:

List out all the products and services you could create from your expert niche.

For each item on that list, decide what stream of income it translates to.

Take a look at what you've created. Is it more active or passive? Is it more physical or online?

Step 5: Proliferate A Consistent Profile

This next chapter is all about preparation for step six. You can think of this step as the hype stage, the stage when you make sure everyone can see you and you're the most easily discoverable person on the planet – fine, that might be a push, but you get my point. Having gone through all the steps so far and having built an audience, you're almost ready to be the establishment in your micro-niche and enjoy all the benefits that come with it.

Right, what does having a consistent profile mean? It all comes back to this concept of a digital footprint. This means that you need to have a presence everywhere possible, all socials, all free platforms and even some of the paid platforms. Even more important than having your profile everywhere is to be consistent. We all have different sides to our personalities and are never defined by one aspect of who we are, however, when we are at the rapid growth phase of building an expert brand, having a consistent profile is the difference between new opportunities coming to you or moving away from you. Furthermore, it's extremely important to achieve organic growth. Allow me to give you an example. Imagine you have a fantastic expert presence on LinkedIn, but on your Facebook profile you're a party animal, wannabe internet comedian and there's no sign of this LinkedIn expert. That's obviously bad, right? Well, you'll be surprised at how often I see this, including myself in the early stages. Not only are you limiting your growth by not taking advantage of a professional presence on Facebook, but you are also sending out an inconsistent and confusing message. As humans, we love things to be consistent and hate mixed messages and when we come across them, we switch off. If you're a dietary expert on one platform, a professional dancer on another, and running for prime minister on another, you will inevitably raise doubt in people and start to create confusion. This, in turn, means that opportunities that people will want to present to you will also be limited as your position as an expert will be doubtful.

Again, what if you want to demonstrate value to more than one audience in two different expert areas? Well, the simple answer is to be active on all platforms with the same amount of vigour you demonstrate for any of your multifaceted skills. What does this mean? Make sure you are a dietary expert on Facebook, LinkedIn and every other platform. It doesn't mean you cannot showcase your sporting or political sides on those same platforms. It simply makes your message consistent across the internet, maximises your growth potential and gives future business partners assurance that you are the bees knees. People often ask me if it's confusing to have more than one presence online, your main job and your expert line. Companies can have multiple faces and still succeed– just look at Virgin and their multiple services.

One point I touched on earlier is this step is like the hype phase. By being an expert and thought leader in a niche you evoke a mini feeling of celebrity. You'll find that no matter the niche, the leaders will often have a sense of celebrity. Consider some of the niche interests you have; now think about the most influential person in that field. You'd probably feel a slight sense of celebrity if you met them in public by accident. That's precisely the feeling you are evoking in this stage and in order for that to happen, you need to have that presence in all the obvious places, as well as the places where your audience likes to congregate. Think about it, which famous athlete, actress or musician doesn't have a presence on most platforms? In fact, I would go as far as saying that many of us validate people's level of fame by their appearance on a Wikipedia page; this is one of the 101 forms of having a consistent profile that is omnipresent. Now, in reality, you don't need to be on every platform ever made, but there are the obvious ones that people expect to find you on and then there are the ones you know your audience are likely to visit. For example, when I was heavily into Cryptocurrency trading, most of the leaders in the area were present on Instagram, Twitter, YouTube, and Facebook but their audience specific platform was Telegram. The same can be said for musicians who would have a presence on Twitter, Instagram, YouTube, and Facebook, but then they would have a presence on a music streaming platform or all of them. The point is that once you cover the main bases, being present on your industry-specific platforms, forums and meetup groups is a great way to grow your status and tap into opportunities specific to that sector.

Another question I often get asked is, "How do I know that my profile is disseminated enough and consistent enough?" First and foremost; most of the world congregate on Facebook, LinkedIn, YouTube, Twitter, and Instagram. How many of these are you on as an expert? The answer should be at least three of them. You should have strong activity on three and though they all have their own merits, if you're strong on three that's normally a good start. The next question I ask HCPs is, have you Googled yourself? A very easy thing to do is Google yourself (the name by which you go including any title people see) and observe what comes up. The first thing that should jump out to you is that the entire first page of the Google search engine should be populated with titles that all say a similar thing, for example: 'nurse Sia, the athlete diabetic footcare…', 'queen of athlete diabetic footcare, Nurse Sia…', 'all you need to know about athlete diabetic footcare' and so on. You get the point. Such a result from searching your chosen name should yield a strong message of your expert status and provide multiple links to where you have been featured in different places. Having a presence on the large social platforms is the easiest thing to do, as people will familiarise themselves with those first, but then your publishing will also kick into effect and people will see the different covers of you, your work, and your opinions. By completing this exercise you've just done what a huge majority of potential fans and business associates are going to do. Are you convinced of your expert status when you search for yourself? If you're not sure how convincing you are, search someone of authority in a similar space to you and see what pops up.

Many of you will find that building a consistent online profile comes intuitively to you and you really enjoy it. For others, it will be quite a challenge. Focus on the places your audience is most likely to be and to share the content you generate. For example, Facebook is a great community platform and many groups thrive well there, so if your content is one that often sparks debate then you should be considering

Facebook strongly. Much of the content you post on one platform is transferable across other platforms. In fact, I rarely change my content to post across different platforms and this makes building a presence very easy, but of course, this doesn't apply to every platform. Take the crossover from Instagram to LinkedIn; it's pretty seamless despite what many think and could give you access to a crowd that you know have a certain educational level and annual income. However, the Twitter audience is far more interactive and a lot more about short soundbites and opinions, so the interaction is completely different. Twitter might best serve your audience if they treat your chosen area as a quick source of information and opinion.

All said, let's recap the main reasons that you need to have a widespread and consistent profile:

1. You are the expert within your niche and have a great pitch and content. You won't maximise your exposure to potential followers until you are present on a multitude of platforms. Remember there are still many who use Instagram, Snapchat and Twitter but are inactive on LinkedIn or Facebook and vice versa.

2. For many who will come across your name, they will run a quick "DBS" check to validate your status. By googling your name, they will expect the results to confirm your expert position. Anything other than this would be a surprise and hugely bring your authority into question. Remember the

journey is similar to that of a celebrity albeit on a much smaller scale.

3. Many of your future opportunities will arise from people running a search on you. Oftentimes, successful networking events, presence on YouTube videos or articles mentioning your name are followed up with a Google search. Think about it, after you watch a film about an inspiring individual or hear a talk you naturally want to Google them to find out more. It's at this point that the consistency of your results (search results that are true to your personal brand) and the plethora of links create a sense of status and authority around who you are. The step after this is the desire for people to want to know you and that's where the final step, step six, comes in.

Summary

Having established income flow in step four, it is time to grow your reach.

Having a consistent brand in multiple online places confirms your "mini celebrity" status.

Make sure you are active on at least three of the big platforms: Facebook, Twitter, Instagram, LinkedIn, YouTube.

Ensure you are present on the more niche platforms aimed at your audience.

Showing multiple aspects of yourself is fine as long as your main brand is aggressively demonstrated across all platforms.

Exercise

Run a Google search of yourself. Are you convinced of your expert status? If not, create a profile on 3 of the big platforms and post something now.

Step 6: Collaborate

And…breathe. We're at the final step of the process. Pat yourself on the back. By this point, you will certainly have established another one or two additional streams of income and have already noticed your lifestyle change. But here's the best part! This is the point at which you get to massage your ego, grow your revenue streams by two to three times and create lifelong associations that will have continued value and give you the platform to influence others as they come along the same journey.

This step could as easily have been called 'partnerships' or 'networking'. It's all about the opportunities that will come to you as a result of what you have done, but even more so, the opportunities you are now in a prime position to create with other people and organisations.

Up until this point, you have been establishing yourself as an expert within your niche and along the way garnered a high trust score and strong visibility. You have been creating value that your fans and business associates will want to access. Leveraging this will amplify all the benefits you've already begun to see.

Collaborating or creating new networks tends to have an intrinsic parity. This means that, while not impossible, it's very rare to see someone who is world famous seek a collaboration with a sole trader just starting up. This just comes down to human nature as we tend to gravitate towards people who are similarly successful, as those networks have a much higher potential to benefit your quality of life. This is one of the reasons that this step comes last because rushing into it will often have you spending plenty of energy creating collaborations and networks with other green shoots. Frankly speaking, this won't augment your income stream or quality of life in any way. You want to be establishing quality partnerships during this process. As I said earlier, you are far more attractive and desirable once you've proven your value in your world. Following on from this, you want to strategically think about the ways in which you can grow your income streams, through partnerships and collaborations. These collaborations can take several forms, let's consider some of them:

Social media influencers – while there is an art to choosing the right influencers or celebrities to associate your brand with, celebrity endorsement has been a thing for as long as anyone can remember and that is because it works. By using either a targeted approach (finding celebrities or influencers that have expressed an interest in your niche) or a scattergun approach (approaching many to see who will be interested) you can often find the influencer who will have an influence over the people you want to reach and at the same time be genuinely interested and grateful for what it is you have to offer. If people believe in what you do enough then often collaborations will be an exchange of services that require no money to be put down. However, sometimes if you know the influencer will have a massive role in increasing your exposure and they are charging, it may be worth paying. Think about how many new customers it would take to cover the cost of that investment and how likely and soon do you project to acquire those new customers/followers. Remember to bear in mind the type of social media influencers or celebrities you choose to endorse you. If your expert niche is foot pain rehab, then it may be less useful having a Disney TV celebrity than it would be having an athlete. Not all endorsements carry the same value, and the bigger the name doesn't always equate to the better the outcome.

Journalists and bloggers – These are great people to have in your collaboration box and often while these people may not be social media influencers, thousands of readers come to their content for advice and guidance. It is sensible to find the writers that could or already have an interest in your area and offer them a piece of your value, either in the form of advice or a service. This allows them to experience your expertise first-hand at no cost and if they like it then they will be motivated to either write about it or introduce you to their editor in chief. Journalists and bloggers have an authority that is very different from social media influencers and celebrities. Think about it, when you read reviews, we often just trust them without really knowing who the people behind them are. There is a type of authenticity we ascribe to written pieces that are composed well and so you may have an entirely new audience waiting for you by associating with the correct writers and bloggers.

Brands – As your status and influence grow, brands will approach you to either review, promote or sell their products through you. As the cosmetic eye doctor, everything from fashion to skincare, to fitness brands have wanted to collaborate with me. It's important that, when you are faced with this, you don't take whatever comes your way as your choice to partner with a brand has a direct impact on your reputation and the way your audience perceives your relationship with them – remember the love is built on trust. Therefore, if you genuinely believe in the brands you choose to collaborate with then you're on the right track. When you do partner up, be sure to make exposure to their audiences a part of the deal. On the flip side, you may identify certain brands that you can see a natural synergy with and crossing over into each other's audiences may provide great value to both parties. For example, since my work was eye focused, one group I decided I would proactively reach out to and work with was Ocushield (a company that creates anti-blue light screen protectors and glasses). At this point, we were both able to identify potential benefits to each other and can now share ideas on the most engaging way to collaborate. Placing myself as an authority in the under-eye beauty space gave me the leverage to confidently build such a network.

Online / Physical Stores – Being associated with certain storefronts brings added credibility, trust and a huge amount of traffic. It can often serve as a gateway to even better collaborations from the other categories. Let's take the following, as an example, if as a part of your process you wrote a book you are extremely proud of, you may want it stocked in a Waterstones in central London. Now, while I have never done this before, I remember having a client who had independently published her book and somehow managed to get her book stocked in Waterstones, Piccadilly Circus. You may not see this as a partnership or collaboration, but all such arrangements are. Both parties are adding value to each other. You may provide a niche book that has potentially high demand and Waterstones will not only elevate your credibility but also expose you to thousands of more potential followers within a year. For many, these things seem like an impossibility, but we're often only ever a few steps away from these pretty astonishing feats. Let's expand on the above example: it's probably incredibly hard to get in front of the shot-caller of Waterstones, Piccadilly. However, through simple research, you may find someone or even ten people who have successfully launched their books there. From there you could approach them on LinkedIn, explain who you are and how intriguing they are to you; most people love to tell their story over a coffee. After having inspected your profile and seeing your accomplishments, one of them may come back to you and you can ask exactly how they found themselves stocked in Waterstones. Such conversations normally end with a friendly rapport built and some ensuing introductions. Before you know it, you may have the ear and even the time of a key publisher or the manager of Waterstones, Piccadilly. You see, this is why I initially said this chapter could easily have been called 'networking'. A basic understanding of how to network and a fearless, tenacious mentality is the key to establishing great collaborations that will hugely impact your success in your niche.

Healthcare professional experts – Other experts similar to you are a great way to collaborate. They say the world is split into three macro niches, within which you will cover everybody; love, finances, health & beauty. So, as a HCP, even though you may not see the initial link, the truth is that by collaborating with other expert HCPs you'll be gaining exposure to an audience that may already prioritise health and beauty. While these people may not make up your early adopters, they can easily become your followers and become key in your growth. Besides this, the network effect of healthcare professionals collaborating often gives people added security and belief in your expertise as it acts as an endorsement from other similarly qualified professionals. Without hesitation, make yourself available to jump on another HCP's podcast or radio show or better still, get them on yours!

Okay, so far from all of this, you can get a sense of the value of collaborations and partnerships and the different groups you may want to target. But, how do you actually go about this? Where do you start from? These were good questions that took me a little time to answer in my personal journey. The first way you may deem the classic way. If you find a marketing or PR expert, one of their initial services will be to create a marketing plan and part of constructing this is to identify who your main competitors are. Now, competitors may be one way of looking at them, but I like to think of them as success examples. Firstly, because you will be in a unique space you won't have any direct competitors, but there will be people in a similar space that are doing well – The 'Joans' if you like. Looking at whom these people have partnered with is always a good starting point as those same partners will be more amenable to working with you since you are in a similar space or have a similar brand. The alternative is to build up what is known as a 'Dream 100' list. This is a list of brands, companies and people you want to work with at some point in the future. This is a list where each of the names can multiply your exposure and/or income streams. This can be built over time and worked best for me by creating an Excel spreadsheet.

The Dream 100 List Template

Over time, you will have built a list with the contact details of key individuals; either their direct contacts or the contact of their managers. The reality is that this game is a numbers game and can take twenty messages to get one response. However, for the most part, writing a short introduction message that can be sent repeatedly is quite straightforward. Furthermore, if you observe the tabs at the bottom of the spreadsheet screenshot, one of the tabs not included is the 'Advisors' tab. These people are some of the most useful. These are individuals who have influence and may have achieved some of the seemingly impossible things you want to achieve. Often, they have already done the hard work of building networks and this introduces the final benefit of having strong partnerships – you save bucket loads of time.

At this point, it's worth remembering what we initially set out to do: create additional income streams, create more time and create greater status all within eight hours a week. Nonetheless, in order to continue staying true to our time commitment, it's crucial you leverage networks effectively. Remember you can use your income streams already planned out in step four to help you decide which types of people you want in your network and any great potential collaborations.

Now that you've got all the juice in terms of how to think and approach this step, I want to give you guys some practical nuggets. You've got an excel contacts spreadsheet with the likes of Harrods, Huda Beauty and all other dream contacts, and you have a strategy on how you're going to reach them. At this point though, you want to be able to populate your spreadsheet with the key information. Here are some steps that were useful to me:

- Finding who the key players and decision makers are can be very difficult, so my experience taught me to search for the following terms via a Google search: 'founders and owners'. They may have sold the company and therefore have more time to dedicate to an upcoming entrepreneur. If that's not the case, they will be an active entrepreneur and will hopefully understand your struggle more than a hired executive. The next term on the search list is 'CEO'. Rarely will they be the one to help you, but if you get their attention, they will ask a member of their team to address your message and when that happens the message will be addressed. Next is a Google search for 'UK director or UK executive'. Obviously, this can be region-specific, but if you're based in the UK this is the one most relevant to you. Sometimes the search will yield articles that detail a former director; don't be afraid to add them to your contact list; they will also have a wealth of knowledge. Once you've found the names from the companies or organisations you're interested in you can use the following ways to approach them.

- **Email**. Finding someone's email can be very tricky but it is the most effective way of reaching someone and getting a response; mainly because the other methods will be subject to so much more clutter and noise. Also, LinkedIn inboxes and Instagram direct messages are not essential for most, so email remains superior. Now, you can just Google search 'name + company + email address' and sometimes, if you're lucky, you'll be given a result. The other, more robust, alternatives are 'ceoemail.com', 'rocketreach.com' and 'hunter.io'. These will give you some useful emails especially when targeting key figures in large establishments. Make sure when sending emails that you attach all your possible social media profiles and any major publications as links in your signature. You want to have the email recipient look into you and be blown away by the strength of your brand.

- **LinkedIn**. This is by far the easiest way to reach people. Most key people of influence will have a LinkedIn presence and you can make twenty to thirty approaches a day. This is done by requesting a connection with a personalised note. That's the way to get your message across without having to wait for your 'connect' invitation to be accepted. Now, bear in mind you have very few words to get your point across because of the limits set, but we will look at this also.

- **Instagram Direct Messages** you may find that you want to approach through a variety of methods, or you cannot find any singular best contact. In that case, using an Instagram approach may be your best answer and it can work. The benefit of this way is that, similarly to a LinkedIn approach, it gives people a chance to cast an eye over your profile before they choose to respond. Having been through all the previous steps, when they glance over your profile they will be impressed.

- Another way which I have personally never done, but I am aware of its success, is to Tweet at your intended target on Twitter. Sometimes, if the message is engaging enough and garners plenty of likes then your target will respond to you.

What you choose to say to your partnership target once you've identified how to reach them is entirely up to you, but you will always face the same struggle – not enough words. You'll either have a word limit or you just don't warrant that much attention, so either way you need to get them intrigued as soon as possible and often that means not focusing on what you want.

Here are some examples of the cold messages I sent.

Hi. I love your brand and what your company is doing. I'm in a similar space and I see the potential to collaborate and bolster our revenues. Would you be interested?

Can I help increase your team's productivity? We spend hours in front of mobile and computer screens, but there's no guide on how to healthily balance eye health and the need to use these devices. This being my area of expertise and the focus of my last book, I'd love to speak with your team about eye health and improving their output.

Hi! I'm being a bit of a fan and I love your products. I'm also aspiring to launch my own niche cosmetic product! I know you're incredibly busy, but you will be helping a young entrepreneur, tremendously, if I could connect with you and hear your journey. I know some amazing coffee spots!

As you can see, they all revolved around two things: how I could help the recipient and the desire to hear their story. These are basic human traits; to gain and be heard. Focusing on these things will give you the best chance of securing a response. The second example was sent to a large company and while I wasn't an eye health expert, as much as I was an eye beauty expert, I was in a position to give advice on some of the bad practices that people in office environments exhibit, since these impact eye health as well as the cosmetic appearance. Sometimes you need to be creative to find your angle and get your foot through the door. These messages are a demonstration of why the previous steps are important. Your collaboration step should have a significant focus on how you can bring value to the table and help the opposite corner's cause. You'll also find that your products, services and content will be some of your most effective networking gifts as you start meeting potential partners. In some cases, as is often the case with advisors (whose knowledge will save you time) your contribution to the relationship may be as simple as access to a new opportunity for them or fulfilling a pastoral desire.

A Note On Saying 'Yes':

Well then, as previously mentioned one of the by-products of successfully making it to step six is that you will be invited to different events, often to speak or teach. From my own personal standpoint, I always find these events useful because they continue to provide a positive feedback loop as you share your knowledge in new environments and have a tangible reinforcement that you are appreciated for what you offer the world. Further to this, these events also represent a great opportunity to foster new partnerships. The likelihood is that if there are other speakers at an event where you are asked to sit on a panel then they are not only influential in their own right but also share some common interest(s) with you; naturally this breaks down barriers and makes networking more organic. It's not rare to go to events and meet figures who would ordinarily be very hard to meet, but due to an attachment to a particular cause, you have the opportunity to bump into them. I found this was the case for me when I was asked to speak at a university event and eventually developed a relationship with another panellist who would later go on to be an investor in my cosmetic eye product.

It's also key to remember that if given the opportunity you should help others in their journey and though you may be at step six there may be another person who is currently trying to move through step three, and your support will be invaluable. Within this journey, everyone moves at a different speed and the not-so-influential person seeking your time now may be a very influential person in eighteen months and the perfect collaborative partner – this process doesn't stop until you choose to no longer be the leader in your niche.

Yet, despite this advice, you still have to be selective when you say yes. Ideally, you would always say yes, but you still have other commitments. If you feel that an opportunity presented to you would diminish, dilute or bring confusion around your brand, then do not be afraid to explore how it could be made more suitable to you or just simply say no. For example, your expert niche may be linked to mental health for single fathers who have a lot on their plate. Potentially accepting to collaborate with a fashion line and being a model may have a negative impact on the esteem of your audience or compromise your image as a person focused on mental well-being as opposed to the image driven culture seen on the internet. So, while being a model may massage your ego, just make sure it's the right move with regard to your fans. Personally, at one point I was asked by a sports brand to do a photoshoot which I thought would be a great idea because eye beauty is still linked to physical health. However, after sharing the photos from the shoot I had a number of new clients express their confusion as to whether I was a medical doctor or a personal trainer. At the time, I thought that was a crazy thing for them to suggest, but the reality is that if someone sees things one way then so do others and it may start to dilute your message and status as an expert in the field; so choose wisely.

You now come to the end of the sixth step; the collaboration step. Designed to multiply all the things you have already built and save you time in the long run. Respect the processes leading up to it and you'll find that the process becomes a smooth one.

A tip: similar to having a consistent and widespread profile, do not underestimate the value of a website, even if it's only one page. You need a landing page; it is crucial as you approach potential partners. Also, make sure you create an official email address. You should already have one at this point, but if you don't, they take ten minutes to set one up. If you don't have a business that trades anything, that's okay, you can create a site with your name.com and an email with firstname@title+first name+surname.com. It need not follow that exact format, but that is a very easy way to come off a little more professional and credible.

Summary

Collaboration is the key to sparking exponential growth, but do not rush to this stage. Rushing to this step will yield unproductive partnerships that won't justify the time spent forging them.

Be strategic and selective in who you collaborate with, create a list of targets – your Dream 100 list.

Partnerships can yield sponsorships, media exposure, direct sales and even advisors. All of these will contribute to a larger audience and greater revenue.

Remember to focus on what value you can bring, not what you can gain.

Exercise

Create yourself some short introduction messages you can send to potential contacts on LinkedIn, Instagram and email.

Build yourself a list of groups or individuals who can help you. Be clear in what way you see them helping you; make those your categories.

Conclusion

Congratulations! You now have the knowledge you need to make a dramatic change to your life as a HCP. The saying goes that knowledge is power, however, knowledge is not power without execution. While you'll find the steps laid out in this book will provide a great framework for you to achieve your goals, the reality remains that even these are useless if you haven't adopted the appropriate mindset. Having already touched on this earlier in the book I won't dwell on it but creating a goal-oriented lifestyle which sets goals on a daily or weekly basis is crucial. You're far more likely to achieve these goals than ones you set yourself over a year. Furthermore, find a group of people or someone that you can be accountable to. You're already busy and so whatever added pressure you can create to help you achieve your short term goals will be of significant value. At the time of writing this book I created a group of HCPs where we would update each other daily on our successes in order to stay motivated. If you can couple this routine with protected time, where you are not distracted by anything, including email or texts, then you will find what seems like small progress initially will be an efficient and impactful eight hours a week.

Another important thing to remember as you go through this process is that you can reflect and improve on previous steps. However, make sure you define clear goals that upon completion will be your cue to move on to the next step; that way you won't be stuck on one step for six months; I've seen this happen. In the same vein, always think about how the fruits of your labour can be used to support your action in the steps to come. For example, sometimes sharing your knowledge or products for free can be a great way to build new partnerships and even incorporate yourself into someone else's offering. I stress this point because as you go through this process you will meet many different kinds of people and entrepreneurs and your question should always be, how can I add value to their life? If you can successfully figure that out in your interactions, then you will find that every step is made easier. We go further together than alone.

This book is part of an ecosystem, 20/20 HCP, designed to support healthcare professionals to discover their expert niche and grow multiple streams of income, create more time and increase their professional status. In order to get the most from this six-step guide be sure to follow the Instagram and LinkedIn pages where there is a stream of knowledge shared regularly. Furthermore, the founder of 20/20 HCP and author of this book, Dr Uche Aniagwu, leads workshops and one to one sessions supporting healthcare professionals to implement the principles in this book, but also provide invaluable templates, guidelines, and expert contacts to help you through the parts of the journey that cannot be broken down into steps. If you are interested in becoming a part of either the workshop or the one to one training then be sure to send an email to druche@2020HCP.co.uk or register on our website, www.2020HCP.co.uk

Success stories are the foundation of the movement we are creating here, so if you've read this book and it's positively impacted your life then follow on the Instagram account @2020hcp and we can feature you on the page and also increase your exposure in return. Finally, there is a Facebook group centred around peer support where useful tips, documents, and networks are shared to help each other's journey. Search '2020 HCP' on Facebook and request to join the group. Make sure you're an active member of the group in order to reap the most from it.

Congratulations on deciding to invest in a better future for yourself. It's the beginning, but I assure you it's a fantastic and rewarding journey. Good luck!

About the author - Dr Uche Aniagwu

Dr Uche Aniagwu MBBS, MSc, BSc had a different route into medicine, and this difference continued through his medical career. After graduating from a Biochemistry undergraduate degree at King's College London, he worked within the Fixed Income, Currencies and Commodities department at Goldman Sachs Investment Bank. It wasn't long into his banking career that he decided that he wanted to do something with a more humanitarian focus and so embarked on a path to Medicine. Before entering medical school, he completed a Master's in Biophysics at Oxford University, and it was there he first discovered his interest in writing, but also principles behind successful businesses and marketing. Being in close proximity to MBA students at the Said Business School, he often engaged in their events and picked up on the key texts that they read; self-educating in the process. By the time he entered medical school he was sure he wanted to be a "doctorpreneur" and with that came the most growth in his career to date. As a medical student he co-founded Rubix, a company that facilitated the corporate social responsibility of G15 housing groups and matched it to the need for free academic tuition from some of the most disadvantaged groups of children in London. This company went on to provide free 12-week courses of Maths and English to over 500 children in London and was later acquired by a larger social enterprise. Concurrently, he co-founded a mobile phone application, Yapnak. The award-winning lunch app gave students access to unprecedented meal deals from top London restaurants whose footfall was lower during the day. It was the first click and collect lunch app of its kind and had over 1,000 active users within the university community. The start-up also enjoyed being part of the famed Barclays Accelerator Community in East London. Dr Uche Aniagwu then made the difficult decision to turn his back on these ventures in order to focus on his foundation years as a doctor, but he was still unable to neglect his entrepreneurial spirit. He later launched Medic Messenger, a mobile phone app designed to replace the need for hospital bleeps and allow the sharing of sensitive patient information. This start-up was a Mass Challenge runner up and secured contracts with University Hospital Lewisham and Queen Elizabeth Hospital Greenwich. By the end of Foundation Year 1, Dr Uche Aniagwu decided that in order to get the best out of his career he would need to be entirely focused on his medical career and as such completed his second foundation year in Kent, without further involvement in the project. By the end of year 2 as a doctor, he had set up a small Rochester clinic offering injectable aesthetic services. This clinic performed averagely, and upon returning to London it became his focus on how to improve his trajectory within injectable cosmetics. It was at that point that this six-step process was born and Dr Uche then followed this same journey. The result? The Cosmetic Eye Doctor. His new brand saw Dr Uche triple his income with one third the time commitment and spawned the first clinic of its kind, a premier teaching course, several major publications, a luxury cosmetic product and a role as a leading doctor within Harvey Nichols' Beyond Medispa.

Dr Uche is still on his journey as the Cosmetic Eye Doctor, but also decided to create 20/20 HCP in order to help other healthcare professionals looking to create more time, more income and have greater job satisfaction. Through his learning, past ventures, and current successes, Dr Uche currently advises HCPs on how to plot their course towards their definition of success.

Printed by Amazon Italia Logistica S.r.l.
Torrazza Piemonte (TO), Italy

13666751R00058